A World Without Circles

A World Without Circles
Copyright © 2012

All Rights Reserved.
No part of this book may be reproduced in any form without permission in writing from the author or publisher.

ISBN: 978-1-935256-28-1

BackDoor Books
PO Box 1652
Boone, NC 28607
(828) 263-9102
ledgepress.com
ledgepress@gmail.com

About the Author: Bethanie Campbell

Writing came early for Bethanie. At six she discovered her passion for writing when the sounds and prosody of language fascinated her. During her teenage years she often found herself lost in a poem by Emily Dickenson or Robert Frost and often running wild with a story by Dr. Seuss. Then, at the young age of 20 came the birth of her daughter, Olivia Grace who further opened her eyes to a world of wonder and words. Crazy ideas, elaborate adventures and splendid characters came rushing to her mind after giving her daughter a bath or playing with her. It was within these moments that she hurried to capture these images on paper.

This excitement with words, ideas and a swelling desire to share her imaginations lead her to finish her Bachelor's degree in Elementary Education. Later she followed with a Master's degree in Reading Education. Her future dreams are for more education and lots of writing.

She writes in moments between being a mom, working at Appalachian State University, tutoring and numerous odd jobs. A great sense of accomplishment comes when she is able to create a story that leaves a lasting impression on readers.

About the Illustrator: Zack Hix

Zack Hix is a 17 year old High School student living in Simpsonville, SC. Drawing has always been a passion, hobby and creative outlet for him. He loves to draw and make cartoon characters and has many books filled with characters that he has created.

Zack and his mom, Kim Hix, started a business in 2010 called Good Boy Roy based on the characters that he draws. They hope to some day make it into a cartoon series and a brand name known everywhere, which is Zack's dream. For now all the Good Boy Roy Characters are on t-shirts and other merchandise. Through this business they hope to share Zack's story of living and struggling with neuropsychiatric illnesses that have and continue to make his life challenging. His story is one of hope and determination, one they want to share with the world. Thankfully, his drawing is opening up fun and new experiences for him. This is the first book he has illustrated, which has been a fun project.

When not drawing or going to school he enjoys fishing, mountain biking, UGA Football, baseball, and spending time with his family (mom, dad, sister Kelsie and 4 dogs–Cruz, Poncho, Maxine and Deuce). See more about Zack from www.goodboyroy.com.

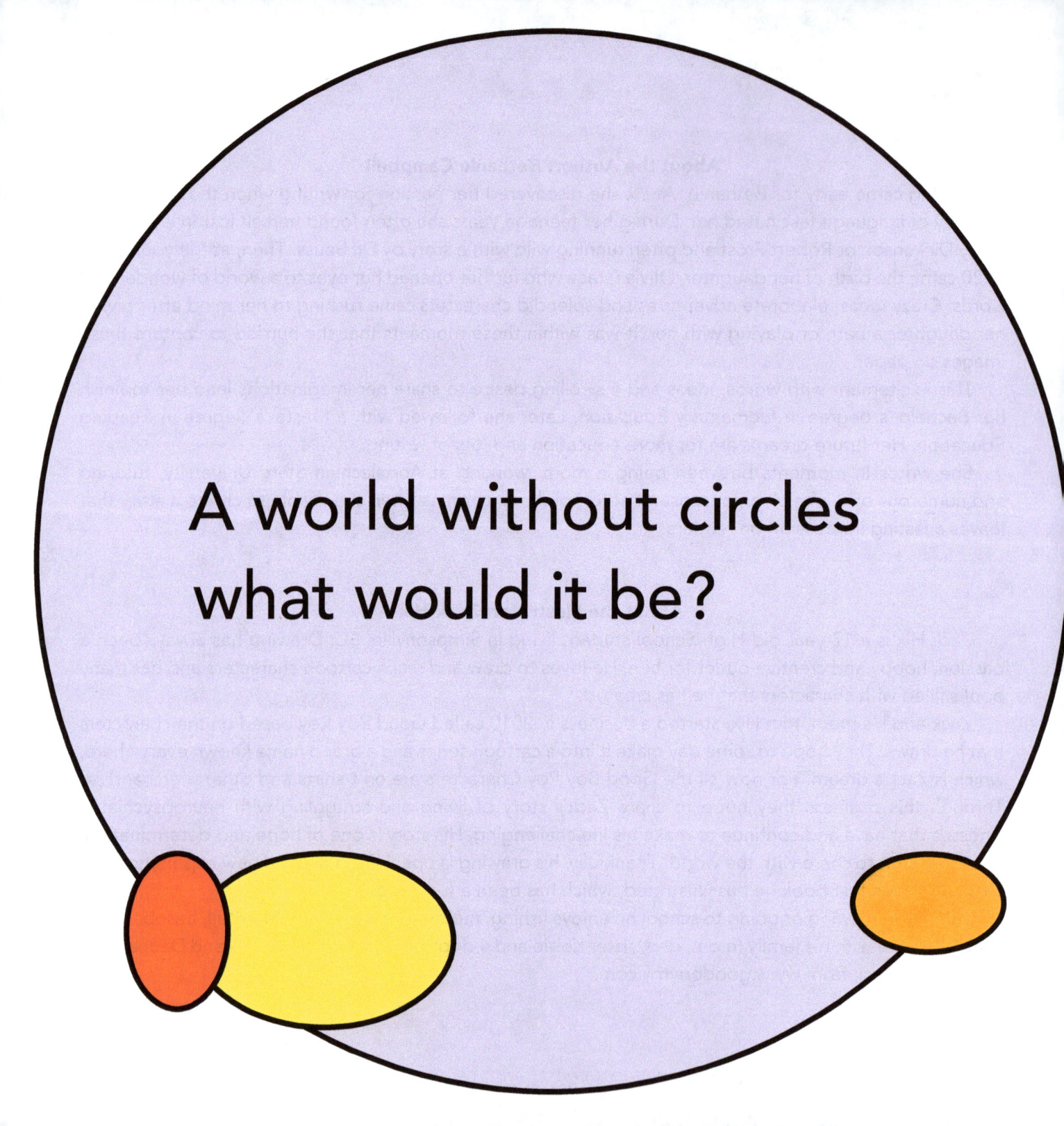

A world without circles what would it be?

There would be no eyes for us to see.

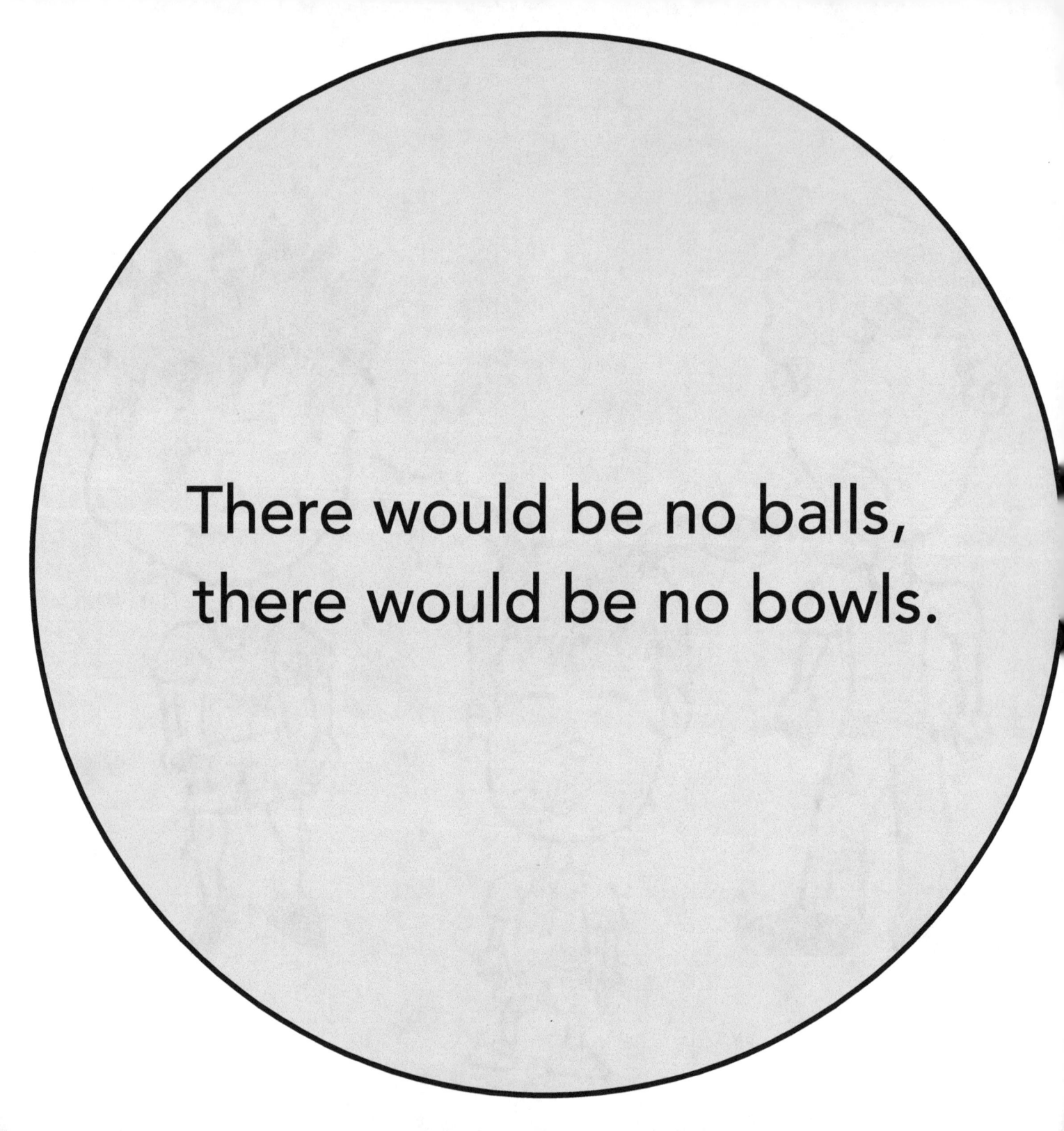

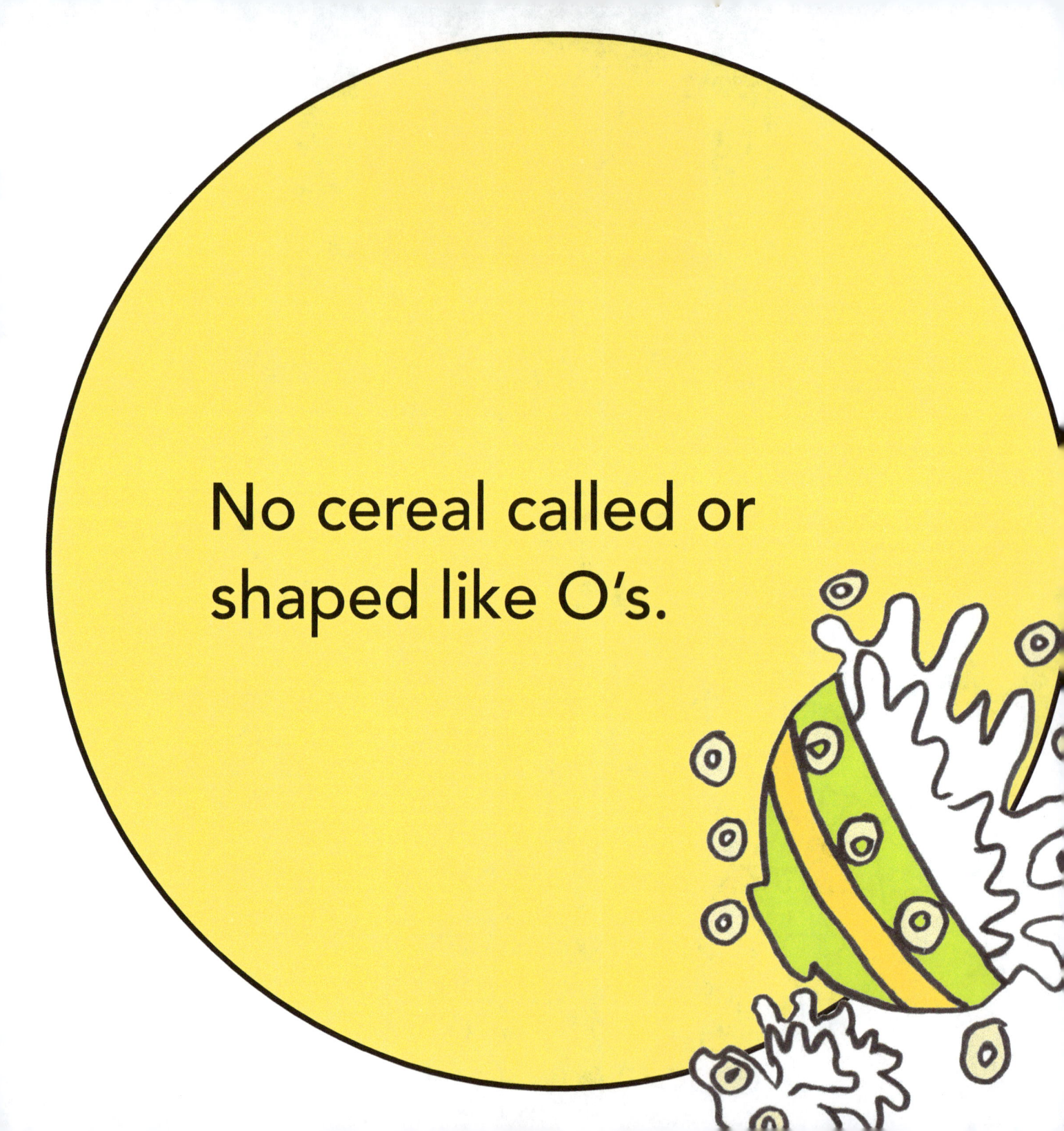

No cereal called or shaped like O's.

There would be no pizza, no pepperoni.

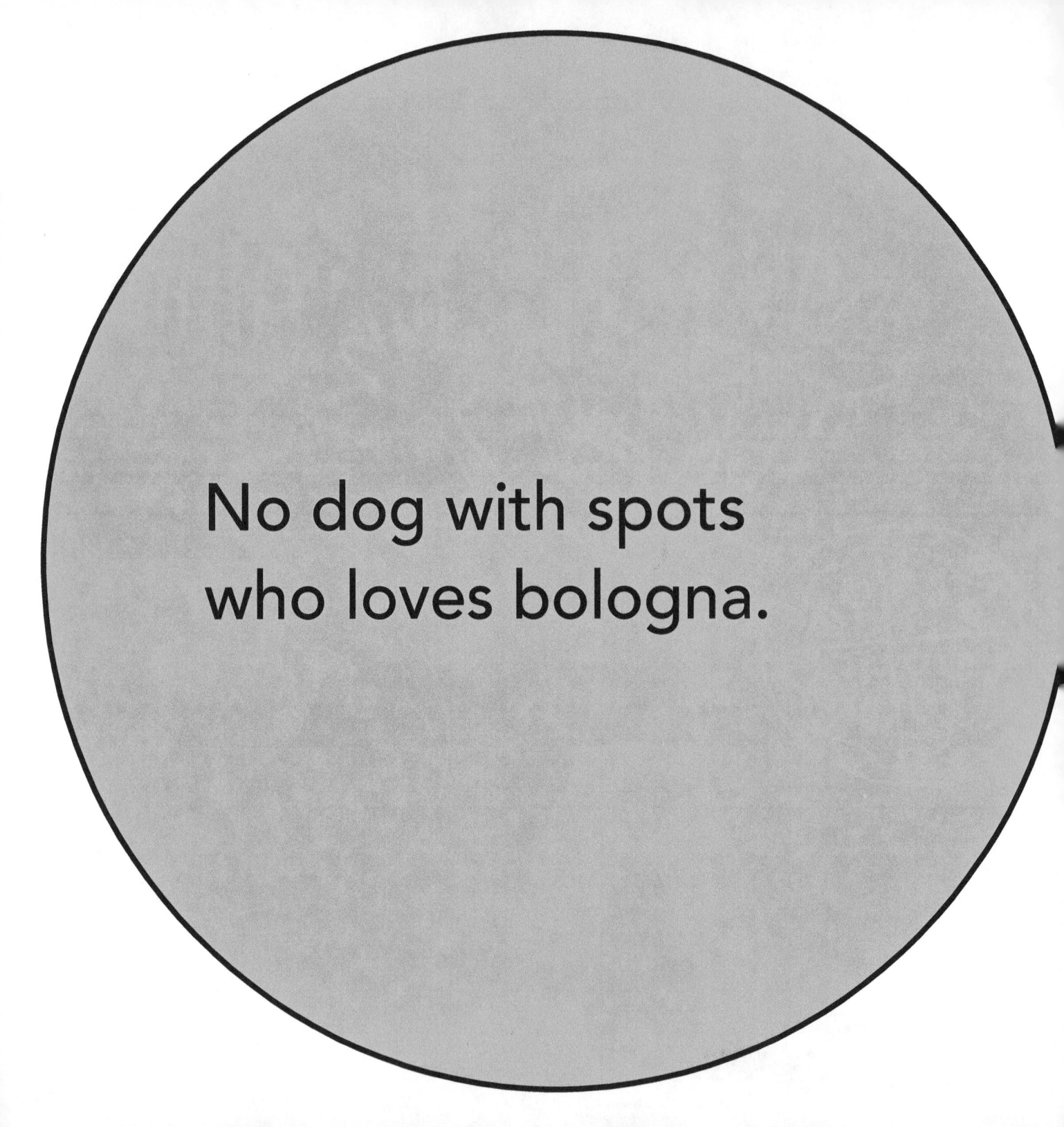

No dog with spots who loves bologna.

There would be no moon to light the sky,

No sun to beam
from way up high.

There would be no checkers, no dominoes.

No globes to find out where to go.

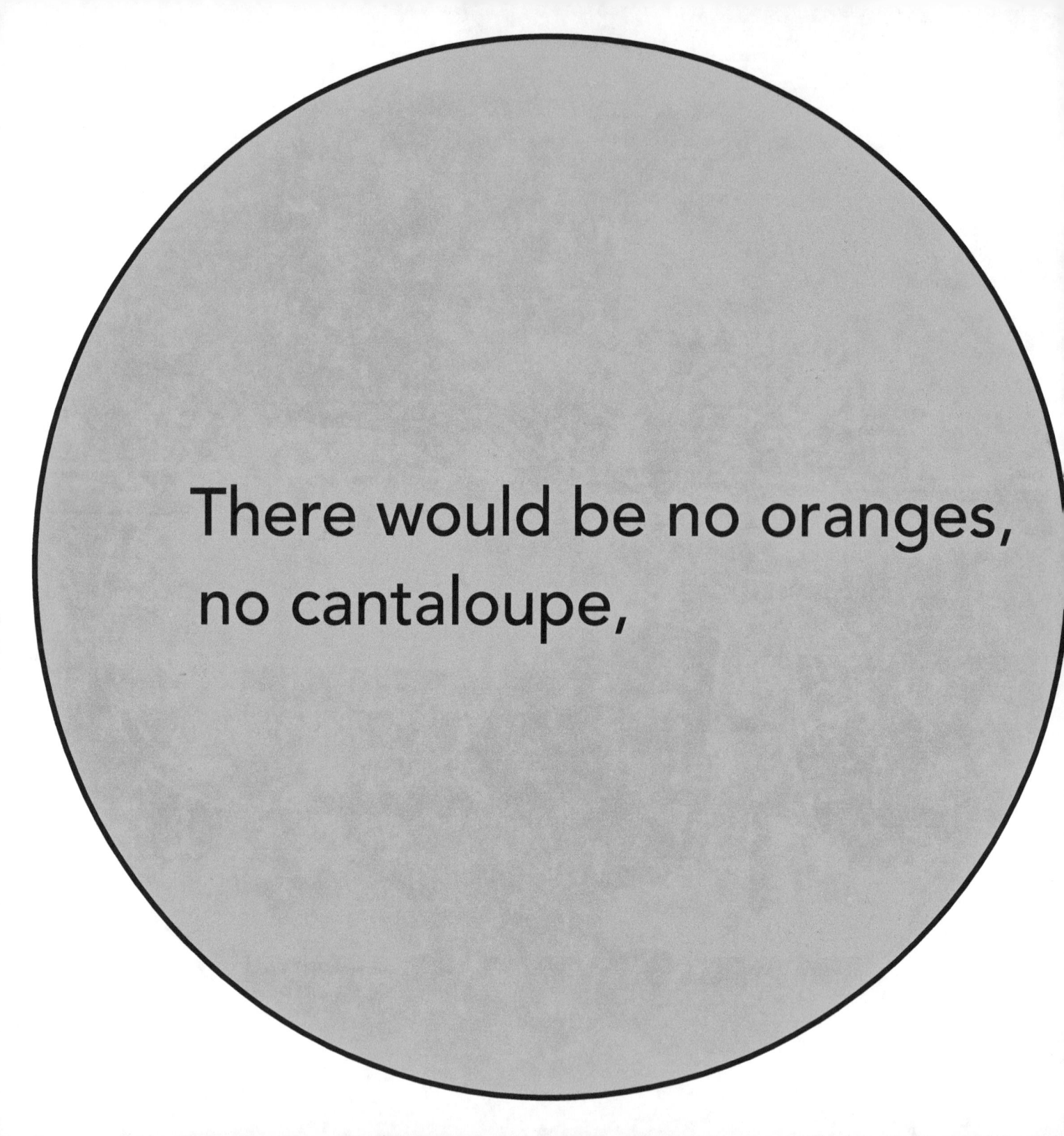

No bubbles made from liquid soap.

A world without circles would be boring indeed.

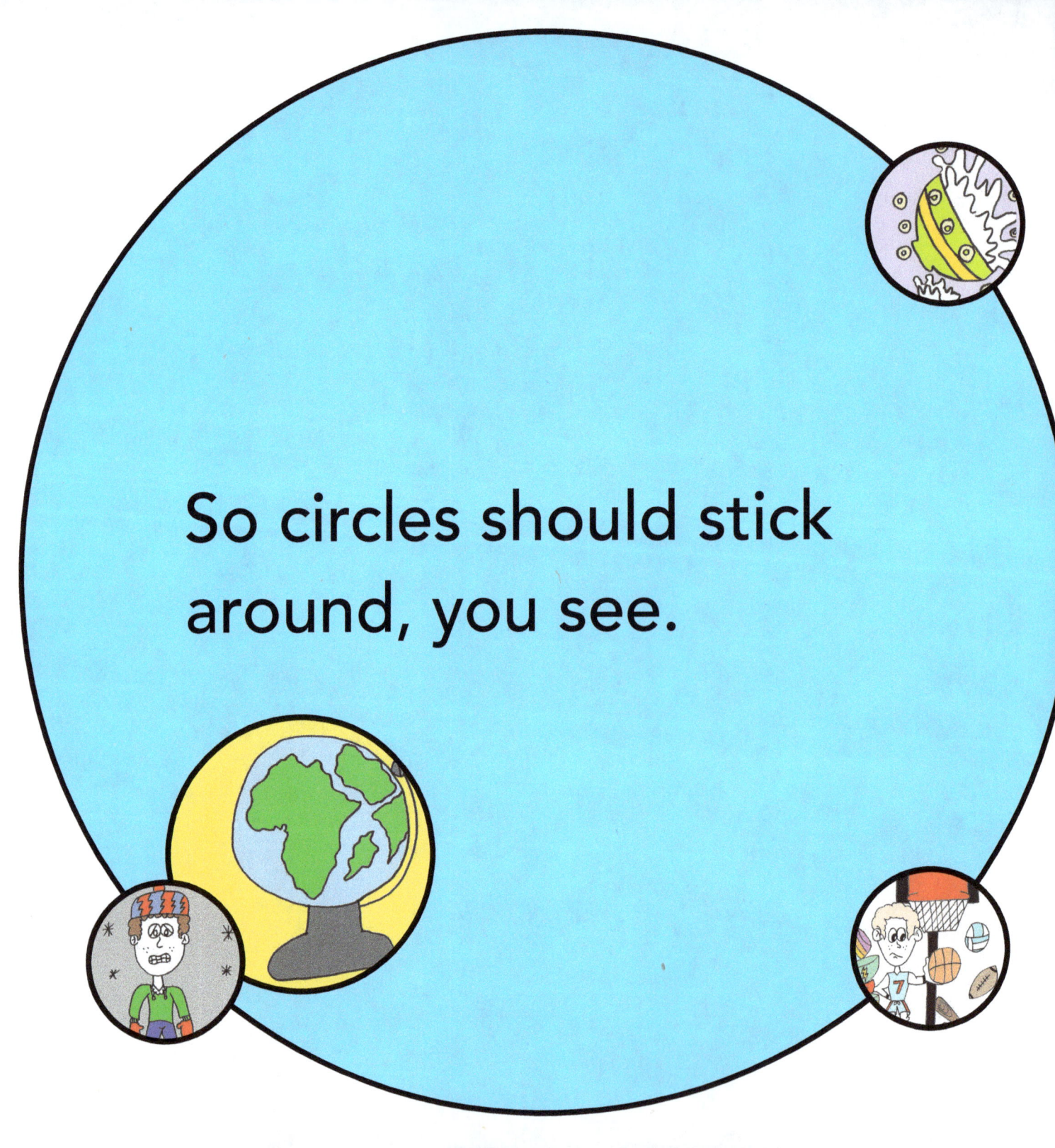

So circles should stick around, you see.

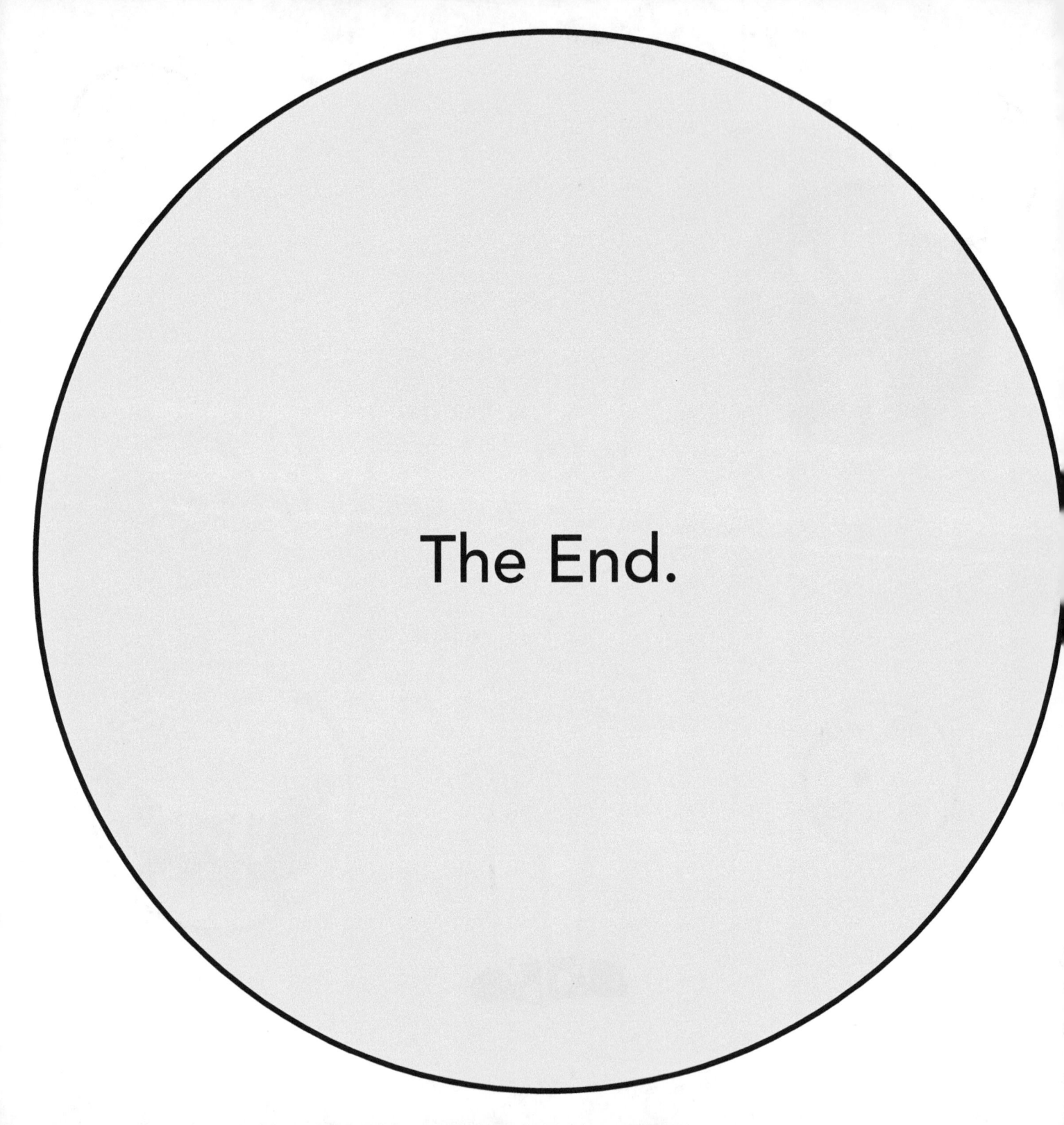